Whispers Of The Wild

The Journey Of A Musher And The Legacy Of Currumpaw Siberian Huskies In America

A True Story

Deborah Abarca Hogan

Paperback ISBN : 978-1-965108-06-2

Dedication

For Currumpaw's Ice Dancer who stayed by me through difficult times, and through her love for me that poured from her eyes. I remembered and wrote her story for all to know so that the Currumpaw pack will live on through the joy a reader may find in this book. To the Chukchi and their sled dogs: For Togo, the greatest of all lead dogs; for the relay mushers of the Nome serum drive and all the huskies from that drive which the native people call "The Great Race of Mercy" that this book will bring back to the modern world that which should not be lost:

In Order of the musher's relay to Nome:

- "Wild Bill" Shannon - 52 miles
- Edgar Kalland – 52 miles
- Dan Green – 28 miles

- Johnny Folger – 26 miles
- Sam Joseph – 34 miles
- Titus Nikolai – 24 miles
- Dave Corning – 30 miles
- Harry Pitka – 30 miles
- Bill McCarty – 28 miles
- Edgar Nollner - 24 miles (Athabascan Indian)
- George Nollner – (Athabascan Indian)
- Charlie Evans – 30 miles
- Tommy Patsy – 36 miles
- Jackscrew – 40 miles (Koyukuk Indian)
- Victor Anagick – 34 miles (Inuit native American Eskimo)
- Myles Gonangan – 40 miles

- Henry Ivanoff – (Chukchi native Siberian living in Alaska)
- Leonard Seppala—and Togo - 340 miles
- Charlie Olsen – 25 miles
- Gunnar Kaasen—and Balto – 53 miles

Special Acknowledgment

I wish to give special Thanks to Brian Crowder for the many hours of editing Denny's book. His wife Elisabeth Renee, who was a good friend and like a sister to Denny, helped me with the pictures and was on the phone with me almost every day, keeping me focused. Our parents, Al and Grace, helped with pictures and the summary about the author at the back of this book. Also last but for sure, not least, Drew Starr & Mike Lansell, who have been so supportive of my parents and myself, Debbie. I know Denny is smiling to see his lifelong friends and family able to work together and get his work published. Brian & Elisabeth Renee of Texas, myself in Washington, and Drew, Mike, and my Parents in Ohio, the miles were not a barrier. Also, I would like to mention the many friends who helped and were there for Denny, as he was there for many of them, each having a different story.

CONTENTS

About the Author

Denny had his book just about done when his life abruptly ended in a motorcycle accident. I, Deborah, his sister completed his book so

my parents and family would keep his legacy living through his book. Before his death, he emailed me his manuscript to read, but before I could give him my ideas, his life was taken Denny was a technical writer and had published several articles in magazines. Even though I wasn't a writer and was in sales, I took on the task of finishing his book.

Page Blank Intentionally

Preface

This is the story of the Currumpaw Siberian sled dogs. It begins with the history of how a tribe of the Chukchi brought them to America. The Chukchi, also known by the name of their larger tribes, the [Luoravetlan] Lygoraveltlat, were the indigenous people who lived in the northeastern part of Siberia, surviving in severe weather with the aid of their amazing sled dogs.

The tale continues with the incredible journey of a legendary musher from the 1920s named Leonard Seppalla, whose participation in the great serum run saved the lives of many children during a diphtheria outbreak in Nome, Alaska. This historic event shows the strength and courage of the mushers and their dogs.

In the present day, this story is narrated by Denny, a modern-day musher, who delves into the history and personality of each dog's role in the pack and on the sled. "This simple story is one of the most precious experiences I have ever had, one that few in the modern world will ever experience. While reading this, please remember that this is not a sad story but a joyous one. It is about a link to the past and a wonderful experience, love and togetherness, the cycle of life, and the indomitable spirit of the sled dog."

Endurance – Fidelity – Intelligence

Chapter 1 – Mush

This is the story of the Currumpaw Siberians. The Currumpaw Siberian sled dogs were named after the legendary Currumpaw wolf and his mate, Blanca. The true story of the Currumpaw Wolf is one of strong and undying love, as wolves mate for life. Hidden in its text is a profound message about the strength of the female and how the male and female of any species complement each other physically and spiritually.

The essence of the Currumpaw Siberians is deeply interconnected with the narrative of Blanca and the Currumpaw Wolf. The wolf, known for his strength and leadership, and Blanca, honored for her elegance and kindness, represent the ideal combination of strength and empathy. The traits of dedication, loyalty, and intellect can be seen in the Currumpaw sled dog history, which bears the history of this renowned couple.

For years, I would tell people stories about the Currumpaws, and they encouraged me to write this book. It was a nice thought, but I didn't think it was something people wanted to read about. In this modern age of movies, computers, and technology, anything seems possible, and this story is a simple one, perhaps no longer meant to be known. The story of the Currumpaws was locked into my memories and held special meaning to me. It would be difficult to write about it in a way that people would enjoy; it would be difficult for me to put so much time and effort into writing something that may not be appreciated.

My feelings on this changed thanks to one sled dog, Blanca. Blanca used to sit outside and let out long mournful howls. Blanca was surely the happiest dog ever, but these sad howls went on every day. Her howls were loud, long, and constantly changing but always seemed to carry a message of sadness.

Blanca's howls rang through the huskies' land each day. I believe there are many reasons she let out these howls, but surely one of the reasons was mourning the passing of what once was — days when the sled dog had a special place in the world, days when they served the thing they loved the most—"the People." Progress and technology have moved society beyond the need for the sled dog. I used to talk to my sled dogs and would tease them about this because it was something they didn't know. In their minds, they served me, and they believed that mushing, the thing they loved to do, was necessary to me. This feeling never left me.

One night, as I stood outside and listened to Blanca's sad songs, somehow, as if she were communicating it to me, I realized she was telling me that there was a story to tell. Though this is the story of the Currumpaw sled dogs, it has a deeper meaning as well - that God sends us our people and gives us the Earth, and we must not turn our back on those gifts, for in doing so, we would be turning our back on God. It tells us, too, that when love and goodness come from within, you will be blessed; that love will cause the shift to good from that which is dark and would destroy us.

This simple story is part of one of the most precious experiences I have ever had, one that few in the modern world will ever experience. All the events in this story are true; I actually had the thoughts I wrote about at the time. While reading this, please remember that this is not a sad story but a joyous one. A story about a link to the past and a wonderful experience, about love and togetherness, the cycle of life, and the indomitable spirit of the sled dog as described on a statue of the heroic lead dog Balto in Central Park, which forever honors them:

"Endurance—Fidelity—

Intelligence"

Chapter 2 – That Which Makes The Chukchi Dog's Spirit Strong

The native people call the sled dogs "spirit dogs." The Chukchi bred their little dogs for over three thousand years and considered them nearly equal to any member of their tribe. For the Chukchi people, these dogs were more than just pets; they were an essential part of their culture and spirituality.

All the Siberian Huskies we see today descended from the original Chukchi seventy-five, the final traces of a vast ancestry. This drastic reduction was a result of the centuries-long wars between Russia and the Chukchi. During these conflicts, the Russians would often force the dog-breeding Chukchi into retreat. When cornered, the Chukchi had no choice but to take to the water in their small boats, risking encounters with their other enemy - the kayak culture Inuit, the American Eskimos.

Each Chukchi family placed their best dogs into the small boats, a testament to the dogs' importance. With limited space, they made the heart-wrenching decision to kill the remaining dogs and even some of their own children to ensure the survival of the sled dogs, the foundation of their culture and means of survival. This profound sacrifice imbued the spirit of the sled dog with a unique strength and bond with the Earth (God). Sadly, the Russians exterminated all of the Chukchi's dogs shortly after the seventy-five were brought to Alaska.

The Chukchi tell a touching story from long ago when famine devastated their tribe and the sled dogs. At one point, only two pups remained. To ensure their survival, a woman nursed the pups at her breast, a powerful act of devotion that preserved the breed.

The Chukchi people have a deep spiritual and cultural bond with their sled dogs, which goes beyond simple practical needs. Pairs were chosen for their qualities and spirit, and useful and spiritual factors influenced breeding and training. Puppies developed solid social relationships because they were nurtured in close contact with people. During training, some customs strengthened the bond between humans and dogs, like Chukchi children sleeping with puppies to create lasting connections.

The Chukchi people saw sled dogs as having a spiritual importance; they thought they shared an essence with the gods and the natural world. Before travels or hunts, rituals such as the "Spirit Dog Ceremony" were carried out to honor and ask for favors for the dogs. This event honored the dogs' contributions and confirmed their valued status in the neighborhood. The Chukchi and their dogs developed a close relationship based on their mutual reliance; the dogs were seen as members of the Chukchi family and as spiritual allies essential to their strength and sense of self.

Chapter 3 – Innisfree and the Chukchi Sled Dog

Innisfree is the most highly regarded Siberian Husky kennel. Kathleen Kanzler, the kennel owner, breeds the finest Siberian Husky show dogs in the world. One of her dogs even won Best in Show at the most prestigious dog show of all, the Westminster Kennel Club show in New York City. The standard to which Siberian Huskies are bred and shown is considered a benchmark in the breeding world. A wise and experienced breeder, Kathleen knew that it would be best for the breed to integrate the Siberian Husky's most distinct and important attribute, the ability to work as part of a sled team, into her breeding program.

The Siberian Huskies were originally bred by a people who lived in the Northeast of Siberia, the Chukchi. They were also known by the name of one of their larger tribes, the [Luoravetlan] Lygoraveltlat. They were people native to the land and, over the centuries, had territorial wars with the other native people in the region, the Samoyeds, who lived to the south, and the Inuit, who lived across the water in the land now called Alaska. The wars left the Chukchi living in the most barren part of the tundra. The barren land, with its harsh weather, left the Chukchi with little food.

To survive, the Chukchi started breeding dogs to pull sleds with which they could travel hundreds of miles to hunt and gather. They became a dog breeding culture, with each generation of young dogs being better than the last. This went on for three thousand years and, according to experts, makes the Chukchi dogs the most pure of the purebred dogs. The result was a small, strong, energy-conserving dog possessing great endurance and the ability to withstand the harsh cold. The Chukchi dogs required very little food, could run fast, and could pull heavy loads for hundreds of miles. They were covered in arctic fur with sturdy guard hairs that shed water and snow, keeping them warm and dry. When the temperature dropped to fifty below zero, the little dogs slept warm and comfortable and would sleep in a little ball with their thick furry tails wrapped around their face.

The Chukchi would also let their dogs sleep in their houses, huddled in their beds to help keep them warm. Legend has it that temperatures at night were measured in terms of the number of dogs necessary to stay warm, giving rise to the expressions "two dog night and three dog night."

The Huskies were also companion dogs for the Chukchi children, who would learn about the nature and instincts of the dogs. These skills aided the children when they reached adulthood. Managing the dog teams was crucial to the survival of the tribe.

The Chukchi dogs came in many colors and had many different types of markings. Many had blue eyes, and some had one blue eye and one brown eye. Some huskies had great big spots or asymmetrical markings on their faces. Others still carried the markings of the king of the Arctic, their near ancestors of the same species, Canis Lupus, the wolf. The Alaskans at the time of the gold rush often referred to the Chukchi dogs as Siberian Wolf Dogs. The wolfish markings became the favorite of breeders, and today, the Siberian Huskies are typified by that look.

Siberians basically come in two colors: red and black. Both color dogs have white undersides and white snouts. If the guard hairs are solid in color, the dogs will have a rich color, such as black. If the guard hairs are tipped in color, then black becomes grey, and red becomes light red. Although many Siberians that are bought as pets are black and white, often with matching blue eyes, the breeders of today do not focus on these colors or even eye color. Most of the Currumpaw Siberians were light red with brownish-red eyes that matched their lips, nose, and the skin around their eyes. Many people thought that they were young wolves because of the light red color of their fur.

For the Chukchi sled dog, life in the village was seasonal. Every spring, the people would let the sled dogs loose, and the dogs would fend for themselves and hunt in packs. To control breeding and the progress of their breeding program, the lead dogs and their breeding stock were kept in the villagesyear-round. All other males were neutered. By being allowed to hunt until these most recent times, there is a wildness instilled in the Chukchi dog that is not found in other domesticated dogs. Huskies are predators and have strong instincts for the order of the pack. They have a passion for the moment and a lust for life because, for the predator, there may be no tomorrow. The predator lives well with heartbreak and suffering.

The predator has a symbiotic existence with nature.

The Chukchi sled dog's journey to America is a story of adaptability and courage. Fur traders and explorers transported Siberian Huskies to North America during the late 19th and early 20th-century gold rush in Alaska. The dogs immediately established their value in the hard Alaskan climate, where their stamina, strength, and teamwork skills were essential for survival. Despite the difficulty of adjusting to a new environment and landscape, the Chukchi sled dogs were able to survive due to their lasting power and adaptability, which date back centuries. Major events like the 1925 serum run to Nome, which saved countless lives by having a relay of sled dogs carry diphtheria antitoxin across nearly 700 miles of dangerous environment, were made possible thanks in large part to their contribution.

The Chukchi sled dogs' introduction to America emphasized not only their remarkable physical capabilities but also their strong spirit and close relationship with people. Its successful integration into American society and the subsequent rise to popularity of the Siberian Husky as a breed in dog competitions such as Westminster are evidence of its lasting influence. Their place in canine history was cemented by the difficulties they overcame, which included long treks and hard winters. These experiences only served to highlight their ability to adapt and survive.

This symbiotic existence is best exemplified by the Inuit story of how wolves were created:

God looked across his Land and saw the need to create another beautiful thing. He reached into a hole and pulled out the Caribou. The Caribou would run in herds and complement the beauty and splendor of the Land. But soon, the Caribou herd became weak, plagued with sickness. God decided that he must create a cure for the Caribou's weaknesses, so he reached back into the hole and pulled out the wolf. The wolf would keep the Caribou strong by weeding out the sick and reinforce the safety the Caribou found in the togetherness of the herd.

Chapter 4 – My Currumpaws

I loved the sled dog and its cousin, the wolf, and believed that if huskies were truly loved and allowed to let their instincts of the pack and its social order mature, I would have a wonderful life with them and that together, they would make an exquisite sled team. To that end, a little puppy was put in a plastic crate, and by car, train, boat, and airplane, it came to me. He was Innisfree's Jim Brandenburg.

Innisfree's Jim Brandenburg: The Noble Leader

Brandenburg was a striking husky with a thick, silver-gray coat that shimmered in the sunlight. His eyes were a piercing blue, filled with intelligence and an unwavering focus. From the moment he arrived, his strength and determination were evident. He was quick to learn commands and showed a natural ability to lead. His instincts in avoiding soft or wet snow made him an exceptional lead dog, always keeping the team on the best path. Brandenburg's dedication and hard work set the standard for the rest of the team.

Currumpaw's Natasha Ko: The Intelligent Alpha

After Brandenburg came to me, the girl I had waited for many years arrived. This was special because her sire, Chrisdon's Triple Bogey, or "Duffer," was rarely bred. Duffer's whelps were the smartest and strongest Siberians with a rare, highly prized, total obedience and attentiveness. This new pup would become the Alpha female, the highest-ranking female of the pack and my constant companion. She would grow to look at me with a love pouring from her eyes, such as I have never seen. She was Currumpaw's Natasha Ko. I would often call her KoKo or Tasha.

Tasha was named after the legendary Ko, and her intelligence was truly remarkable. When people would stand around talking, Tasha would struggle to understand the conversation, her head tilting side to side out of frustration at not being able to comprehend every sentence and word. Brandenburg loved Tasha, and she loved him. Theirs was a perfect love, a love so rarely seen. I would have envied them if it weren't for the great love they would come to show me. Of course, regarding love, they were Currumpaws.

Blanca: The Joyful Omega

Following Tasha came Blanca, making the same trip as Brandenburg, hand-selected to be a perfect mate for him. Blanca was the epitome of joy and resilience, with a fluffy white coat that made her look like a snow angel. Her eyes sparkled with mischief and kindness, and she quickly embraced her role as the Omega female, the lowest-ranking member of the pack. Despite the challenges of her position, she found joy in every task, bringing a light-hearted energy to the team.

I trained the three huskies to pull their sled. At first, I trained Brandenburg to respond to left and right commands, gee and haw. I teamed the three dogs with Brandenburg, and Tasha hitched next to each other in the lead positions. Blanca worked the wheel position closest to the sled alone. Natasha, with her innate desire to respond to my wishes, quickly learned the role of the lead dog from Brandenburg. They would compete to see who could respond most quickly to my commands and who could figure out difficult directional changes first. Brandenburg was a great lead dog, always working hard and never stepping in soft or wet snow. Brandenburg had a wonderful ability to lead the small team.

Chapter 5 – Every Currumpaw Morning

As I was sleeping one morning, I was awakened by the most disturbing sound: a loud combination of a whelp, a moan, and a scream. Innisfree's Blanca of Currumpaw (Blanca) water had broken, and she was giving birth. I went to see Blanca after she made that horrible sound and sat with her for many hours. It was the first and only time I ever experienced birth. The first to be born was a solid red female. When she grew, she followed me around everywhere, looking up at me with her big brown eyes—she seemed to love me. She was spunky, and I called her Stormy. Then came a very white female, light red as we say, but her hind legs came first. She didn't pass easily, but I learned what to do and eventually grabbed her hind legs and pulled her out. I called her the Wrong Way. As Wrong Way grew, she became uncommonly dainty and pretty. This wonderful pup soon came to be known as Pretty and, eventually, Ici.

I had to sell most of the puppies because I didn't really have room for them all. I wanted them to have good homes. Pretty was such an attractive puppy that she was quickly taken home by a pro football player named David, who wished for his three-year-old son to grow up with a nice dog. A few days after I sold the puppy named Pretty, David, her new owner, came to my home and sadly returned the little puppy because his wife didn't want to deal with the mess the baby Siberian might make of their home. That night, I went to bed, and Pretty crawled into bed with me, falling asleep over my right leg. I could never part with her again. Pretty would sleep over my right leg for most of the rest of her life. In hindsight, I believe there were many reasons beyond fate for Pretty's return to me. By coming back, Pretty would have the chance to live a life very different from that of a simple family pet. She would grow to be a sled dog and inhabit a very special place in my life. David had changed Pretty's name to Ice, and upon her return, I renamed her Ici. She is Currumpaw's Ice Dancer.

Ici is a little, red female Siberian Husky, but unlike the Siberians, we often see proudly walking with their owners, riding in their cars - Ici is a sled dog. Ici's fur is almost pure white, adorned with guard hairs tipped with light red. Like most red Siberians, her lips, nose, and eyelids are a liver color and match her eyes. Ici bears a stunning resemblance to a little lead dog named Togo, who lived in the 1920s.

Blanca would have two more puppies that night.

After Pretty came to the "monster puppy," distress and horror, it was too big to pass, and Blanca would surely die. But I used all the tricks I learned to help her. After a long time, the puppy came out, but it was dead from having its umbilical cord squeezed in the birth canal for so long.

After Blanca delivered the still-born monster puppy, out came another light red girl. This little cinnamon- colored girl was behind the monster puppy and stuck in the birth canal for a long time. She, too, was limp and lifeless. The little lifeless puppy just covered the palm of my hand. She felt heavy, but I thought perhaps it was not too late. I rubbed her heart over and over and blew into her mouth - seemingly forever. How sad I thought she was gone - I kept rubbing her heart anyway, blowing air into her mouth, her little lips spreading as the air passed in. Suddenly, she came to life! Somewhere in her unconsciousness, she fought and fought for life. The little cinnamon girl quickly recovered from her difficult birth and was thriving—she was a survivor.

Later, I realized that this little cinnamon girl must stay. She would grow to be the strongest sled dog I have ever seen. She was protective of me and her pack and lived with a lust for life like no other. The rest of my time with her, I would be in awe of her. This feeling never left me. She was Leto, Currumpaw's Leto. Leto's name came from the godmother of Mercury. Losing favor with Zeus, Leto had lived her life as a wolf to hide from his anger.

After Leto's birth, I wrapped the monster puppy in a towel and respectfully laid him in a safe place near the whelping den. I looked at the still little puppy wrapped in the towel. I noticed that his face had that cute look that newborn puppies have, a sort of helpless expression with their eyes closed tight. I thought of the fact that this little one would miss all the pleasures of life, running with other huskies, being loved - love returned from the people he would have loved with all his heart and soul. I realized that the little dog should have a place to rest fit for what he was born to be, a Chukchi sled dog.

After resting, I placed the puppy's body in the dog bag on the sled. I hitched up Brandenburg and Tasha to mush the puppy to a peaceful place far into the woods. We stopped at a location just thirty feet from a beautiful trail that runs along a stream. A trail that my sled dogs would run with pure joy— they were perfection in motion. I buried the puppy there in this place where my team would occasionally mush by so that even after death, perhaps he could feel the joy of what it was to be a Currumpaw.

Before the puppies were born, I built a whelping den. A special warm place where the puppies would be born and where Blanca could go in and nurse them. The whelping den was built to keep the puppies in and allow Blanca to leave the den so as to get her much-needed space away from them so she could recover from nursing. Only days after the puppies were born, I would wake in the morning to find Leto out of the puppy den, nursing alone on an annoyed Blanca. Leto was yet unable to walk, and Blanca certainly would not pick her up and move her out of the den, so how did she get out? One night, I spied on her. Leto crawled up to the dividing board that kept the puppies in, rested, and then pushed her little body up the side like a snake until she could get her little elbows over the top. Exhausted, she rested, hanging there by her elbows. Then, in one last big effort, she would pull herself over the top, falling onto the floor with a loud plunk. Then, she would crawl to Blanca and nurse alone the rest of the night. This would be her way for the rest of her life, fighting to run fastest, experiencing all that the world had to offer, and showing me how precious life was.

During the serum run to Nome, dogs freeze on their feet while mushing—it is this spirit that makes the Chukchi dog strong. Leto would gladly have frozen on her feet, if necessary, to help the lead dog bring the team home.

Leto would power the team in races. They were so fast that in their first major race, a race that is normally decided within seconds between teams that came from across the country, the Currumpaw Siberians won with a lead of over eight minutes.

Leto and Ici were best friends, always causing mischief and bringing joy with their antics as puppies. Leto grew up to be the protector of the pack, alerting them to danger when an intruder tried to enter the house one snowy evening. She loved watching TV, especially shows with animals, even though she knew they weren't real. Leto and her mother, Blanca, enjoyed playing outside together, engaging in games like "King of the Mountain" and "Wolf tag," which were typical husky fun.

Chapter 6 – Sep, Togo, and the All Alaska Sweepstakes

The Siberian Huskies we know today trace their ancestry back to a group of seventy-five dogs brought to Alaska in the 1920s from Siberia by the Chukchi people, who had been breeding them for thousands of years. These dogs were initially brought to Alaska to compete in sled dog races like the All Alaska Sweepstakes. During the gold rush, Alaskans, flush with wealth but isolated by the lengthy journey back to the lower forty-eight states, found entertainment and competition in dog sled races. These races, with their substantial cash prizes, became known as "sweepstakes," reflecting the sizable sums involved.

Leonhard Seppala, affectionately called "Sep," arrived in Alaska and quickly established himself as a prominent figure in sled dog racing. He was among the first mushers to race the Siberian Huskies, commencing his breeding program with his dogs Dolly and Suggen. Despite his diminutive stature, Sep's prowess on the trails earned him respect, even as he became known as "the little man with the little dogs."

Among Sep's breeding endeavors was the union of Dolly and Suggen, resulting in a solitary offspring, a small male named Togo. Initially, Sep doubted Togo's potential as a sled dog due to his size and mischievous nature. However, Togo's intelligence and affinity for Seppala undeniably led Sep to recognize his worth as a working dog.

Despite attempts to rehome Togo, including a stint on a farm, the spirited pup repeatedly returned to Seppala's dog yard. Eventually, Sep relented and allowed Togo to remain.

Togo's escapades continued during one of Sep's absences on a three-day journey to Dime Creek. Despite being confined to a kennel, Togo managed to free himself, sustaining injuries. His determination to join Sep's team on the trail led to an unexpected encounter, where Togo's presence initially startled Sep.

Sep saw Togo's determination and work ethic and integrated him into the sled team, eventually establishing him as a lead dog. Togo's quick grasp of lead orders and steadfast determination pushed Sep and Togo to victory in sled dog races, including the famous All Alaska Sweepstakes.

Chapter 7 – Togo's Run: The Greater Race of Mercy

On January 20, 1925, a desperate telegraph call rang out from Nome, Alaska: "Nome calling... Nome calling... We have a diphtheria outbreak... No serum... Urgent assistance needed... Nome calling... Nome calling..." The city was facing a deadly epidemic amid the harsh winter conditions of Alaska.

The necessary serum was over a thousand miles away in Anchorage, but the heavy snow and extreme weather rendered airplanes useless. The open-cockpit planes couldn't withstand the conditions, and even if they could, the engines were frozen. With no other options, the city faced the grim prospect of losing its children to the disease.

Anchorage received the distress call and located 300,000 units of serum at a railway hospital. The package weighed 20 pounds and could be shipped by train to Nenana, where it could potentially be transported to Nome via the Iditarod trail using dog sled teams.

Leonard Seppala, with his renowned lead dog Togo, was one of the mushers selected for the task. Seppala and Togo pressed on relentlessly Despite setbacks and treacherous conditions, including deep snow and sub-zero temperatures. The trail disappeared in the whiteout, but Togo's instincts and Seppala's trust in him guided the team safely.

Togo led the team across the dangerous Ice of Norton Sound, cutting over a hundred miles and a full day of travel from the return journey. Their timely arrival saved Nome from further devastation. Togo's heroic efforts, however, took a toll, leaving him permanently lame after covering over three hundred forty miles during the drive.

Despite Togo's significant role, the story of the serum run often focuses on Balto, another lead dog on a different team. While

Balto's team finished the final portion of the journey to Nome, Togo, and Seppala covered the expedition's most challenging and risky stretches.

Senator Dill of Washington immortalized the serum run in the Congressional record, highlighting the unparalleled speed and endurance displayed in the face of a crisis where humanity and life itself were at stake.

Chapter 8 – Of Innisfree's Jim Brandenburg

I often referred to Brandenburg as "Buddy," the sole male among the pack. He was a large husky with a stunning coat of thick white fur accented with strawberry-orange tips on his guard hairs. Aloof and proud, he preferred to stay close to me, showing little interest in others. His days were often spent gazing adoringly at Tasha, his eyes half closed in a smile. While Tasha took charge of the other huskies, he would often prance around in a playful manner, his gaze fixed on her. When Tasha approached him, wagging her tail, they would touch noses as if confirming her status as the most beautiful sled dog.

Brandenburg seemed perpetually content, often seen sitting or standing with a half-closed smile, a sign of his carefree and submissive nature. It was evident that he believed everything in life would always be alright. His days were filled with the companionship of the Currumpaws, exhilarating sled runs, and the breathtaking beauty of nature on his land. He found joy in observing the antics of the other huskies, particularly the four females, all while deeply enamored with Tasha. His happiness was infectious; merely looking at him filled me with joy, for in Brandenburg's eyes, life was perfect.

In his youth, Brandenburg and Tasha comprised a two-dog team, leading sled runs along a secluded six- mile trail by the river. I personally trained him to lead, and he quickly mastered the skills, passing them on to Tasha and Ici. Unlike other working dogs, lead dogs learn best from their peers, understanding commands like "haw" and "gee," scenting out the trail, and ensuring the team's safety. A skilled lead dog always brings the team home safely.

However, as Brandenburg aged, he ran less frequently. One night, during a sled run, he suddenly stopped after covering only half a mile. Intuitively, I knew something was wrong; something was causing him discomfort, and he understood it was best to cease running. I placed him in the dog bag, carried on the sled for such occasions, and we returned home.

It was later discovered that Brandenburg had epilepsy, explaining his reluctance to continue running with the team. With Tasha and Ici taking over as lead dogs, their learning continued through friendly competition. Ici, aware of Tasha's favored status, competed with her to execute commands swiftly and proudly, always aiming to please me.

Chapter 9 – A Day in the Life of a Currumpaw

The antics and expressions of the huskies were priceless. They laughed, expressed joy by running in a rocking horse gait, and at play, their facial expressions ranged from taunting to defiance to outright silliness. They would talk to each other in rolling tones and make silly faces—their love for each other was so apparent.

Standing with the huskies on their land, I felt overwhelmed by a sense of togetherness. Each husky would look me in the eye with expressions of pleasure, love, and adoration. To them, I was the most wonderful sight. Each looked at me fittingly to their personality; sweet Brandenburg stared with half-closed eyes, smiling; Blanca wagged her tail wildly as if saying, "Aren't I cute? Come pet me!"; Leto, the warrior, showed pride and respect; Ici had a stoic, concentrated expression, the aloofness of a true sled dog. And then there was Tasha, who gazed with absolute adoration, her perfect little feet covered in thick fur, looking like stuffed animal feet.

The huskies were bred as show dogs, evident in their gait. They moved perfectly, head held high, ears pointed up, with a prideful gait not usually seen in other breeds. It seemed like they floated rather than walked, moving efficiently and effortlessly, translating into speed and endurance on the trail.

Their favorite game was wolf tag, full of athletic moves to dodge the pursuer and funny faces they made at each other. I would watch them play for hours, often laughing hysterically as one husky would sneak up on another, tiptoeing up behind and scare it with a great pouncing leap. The other husky would turn, embarrassed, and the pursuit would start again, often with each of them laughing and running in that silly rocking horse gait.

The huskies also knew how to play alone. A favorite solo game was grabbing a toy—anything from a rawhide bone to a piece of bark—

and stalking it, pouncing around it in circles, woofing at it, and finally attacking it. Then the husky might grab it and run off, throwing it up in the air and catching it, sometimes missing and pretending to be surprised, starting the stalking all over again.

The huskies received plenty of affection from each other and from me. Living with the Currumpaws was a loving experience, so much so that I would sing little songs to them, celebrating their lives. Each husky had their own song, and they loved it when I sang to them, repeating their names over and over. It may be hard for people to understand, but in song, like singing in church, your soul opens, and your true feelings and heart come out. The huskies loved me more for it.

Brandenburg's song was beautiful and sad, to the melody of Edelweiss. Tasha's was silly: "Tasha KO, Tasha Ko, pulls a sled, any size, Tasha Ko!" Blanca's was equally silly, sung to the melody of Casper the Friendly Ghost: "Blanca the friendly dog, the friendliest dog we know, Blanca paw, Blanca paw, Blanca, Blanca, Blanca paw."

For Leto, it was a rough, masculine song I once heard in a Star Trek movie, a Klingon melody. Leto, a great warrior, loved it. Ici's song was simple, stating her name over and over: "Ici the Ice Dancer, Ici the Ice Dancer, Ici the Ice Dancer, Ici—Ici—Ici."

I would pet the huskies often and hug them, wrapping my arms around their thick ruffs, lifting and squeezing them so that their forepaws lifted off the ground. This pleased them and reinforced my place as the master of the pack.

Most mushers raise their dogs in a dog yard, each dog staked out with a dog-house for privacy and warmth. The Currumpaws, raised as a pack and sled dogs, were also pets. They slept in the house with me, enjoying their togetherness and being near their master.

The Currumpaws developed a large vocabulary and responded to many commands, including hand signals. One of the most fascinating things was how they responded appropriately without commands.

They liked to go in and out of the house to play or do their doggy duties. I could walk to the door, and any husky wanting to go outside would follow. They spent time in a kennel room when I was away, and when it was time to leave, I would walk toward the kennel room, and they would all follow, each going into their individual kennels, smiling at me.

The huskies were trained to have house manners, behaving differently inside than outside. Outside, they could play and do anything they wanted, but inside they behaved well because they loved the togetherness. Huskies naturally conserve energy, spending their time in the house relaxing and sleeping. The Chukchis kept their best huskies in their homes, and the huskies' instinct to be compatible with human life made them perfectly suited to living indoors. As I walked around the house, a group of huskies followed me everywhere—how comical that must have looked to visitors.

They loved watching dinner be cooked, huddling around my feet, never getting in the way. They never begged for food from the table, knowing food never went from the table to a husky. Allowing that might lead the pack to take over. They sat attentively while I cooked, waiting for scraps. Leto especially liked catching lettuce leaves I tossed while making salads, shaking them violently before eating them.

Chapter 10 – Any Morning—Any Day

Each morning, the huskies would wake, and Tasha would celebrate the day as she did every day—letting out a big moan to let her huskies know it was time to get up. She would jump in the air with a half twist and a big smile, then roll on her back, wiggling and scratching. Finally, she would lay there on her back and watch me—upside down.

After breakfast, I would relax for a moment. Without a word or action from me, hysteria would break out; the huskies somehow knew I was thinking about taking them mushing. How did they know? It's a mystery to this day. This is how it always was, any time, day or night.

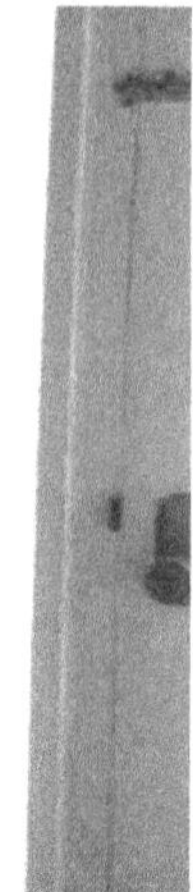

The huskies loved living in the house as much as they loved spending time outside. They enjoyed watching the day-to-day activities and relished our time together. They would run outside with great enthusiasm and return just as excited. They were perfectly suited for the cold or rain, but they loved the house too.

One day, the temperature dropped to forty below zero, a rarity in this temperate land. Brandenburg wanted to go outside in the dog yard, so I let him out. He walked through the snow into the bitter cold, with the wind blowing strong and setting a chill factor far below one hundred degrees below zero. After a short while, I called for him to come back, but he was standing far back, gazing over his territory. I checked on him several times, but each time he wanted to stay out. With these cold temperatures, I began to become concerned about him. I called for him once again, and he just looked over at me and didn't budge. I decided to go out and get him.

I walked to the back of the huskies' land where he was standing. There he stood with the wind in his face, a great big smile, and his eyes half closed. He didn't want to come in because these bitter temperatures were unusual for us, and standing out there must have sparked something in his instincts. He just stood there smiling. What was he thinking? I imagined he was just enjoying the bitter cold, the howling wind, and blowing snow, and thinking to himself, "This is perfect; this is home."

I touched him gently on the back of the neck, a dominant gesture the huskies were accustomed to, meaning they should follow me. He immediately went with me into the house. Once inside, he walked up to a window and stared outside for a very long time.

Spending so much time with the huskies put me in touch with their thoughts and feelings. But this demonstration of Brandenburg's attraction to the bitter cold was one I will never truly understand; I can only guess. The Chukchis called the little dogs "Spirit Dogs." Perhaps Brandenburg knew that this harsh weather, so threatening to human life, was where the little Chukchi sled dogs shined. Weather like this had created times throughout history when the little dogs were the last hope for the People. In these times, the sled dogs stepped up and made great contributions to the survival of the Tribe.

Chapter 11 – Any Evening—Any Night

The night is late, and it's time for bed. The five Currumpaw Siberians file into my bedroom, each with its own special place: Tasha sleeps on the floor next to me, Brandenburg by the door, Blanca in the corner, and Leto on the far left corner of the bed. Ici sits on the opposite side of Leto, on my right. Ici sits there with her chin up and an annoyed look on her face, waiting for me to get into bed. Once I finally slip under the covers, she stretches her neck over my right leg, laying her head down with a great big sigh and resting it there for the rest of the night.

The silence? Not quite. Each night, the room fills with the soothing concert of the huskies' rhythmic breathing. It's a comforting sound that lulls me to sleep, reinforcing the bond of the pack. The Chukchi people believed that a man's wealth was demonstrated by the quality and love of his sled dogs and the team. As I drift off to sleep to that rhythmic sound, I often think to myself, "Who could be richer than I?"

As I lay there, surrounded by my huskies, I reflect on the sense of peace and contentment they bring into my life. The quiet moments before sleep are filled with a deep sense of gratitude for their companionship and loyalty. The gentle breathing of the huskies is a nightly reminder of the bond we share, a bond that transcends words and is rooted in mutual respect and love.

Occasionally, I watch them in the dim light, each lost in their dreams, with twitching paws and soft whimpers. These serene moments, enveloped by the warmth and companionship of my huskies, make every night feel like a blessing. Their presence is a constant reminder of the simple joys in life, and as I fall asleep, I am filled with a profound sense of happiness and fulfillment.

Chapter 12 – The Complete Sled Dog

The social order of the pack is strong, with each member having a special and important place. As civilized humans, it is difficult for us to relate to the culture of predatory animals. Predators have their own unique needs, unlike ours, and they fight. Even today, with the knowledge of field biologists and other scientists, we still try to anthropomorphize animals and impose our desires on wild animals, regardless of their nature. Civilized man is, for the most part, more ignorant of nature and wildlife today than at any other time in history.

Recently, people began taking on wolves as pets and breeding hybrid wolves, which are part dog and part wolf. Breeders have promoted their breeding as being a certain percentage wolf, as if it were some attractive quality. The wolf is wild and has no place with humans. We can certainly share the land with the wolf, but it is not in our or the wolf's nature to cohabitate with each other. People buy these creatures as pets, which usually leads to the creature's demise when the owners start experiencing all the uncivilized parts of the wolf.

Wolves need a vast amount of land to sustain themselves and are not comfortable living as we do. Keeping a wolf on a plot of land, even a spacious forty-acre spread, would be akin to raising our children in a closet. An inevitable neurosis develops, soon followed by the demise of the animal. This attempt at domestication creates an emptiness in the lives of captive wolves—the unfulfilled desire to live as a wolf.

Wolfers and native people have nothing good to say about this practice. Native people, who are close to the land and nature, find it incomprehensible to confine what is meant to be free. Wolfers, those who hunt wolves for bounty, must understand wolves to be successful. While I do not approve of wolfing, it has always been government-sanctioned, and we must recognize people for their skills and knowledge. Native people cannot comprehend why anyone would want to confine what is free, preventing it from doing what it was meant to do: live with the pack, hunt, sustain the pack through time, and be one with Nature.

Regarding the percentage of wolf in a hybrid, wolfers say, if it acts like a wolf, it's a wolf. The difference between wolves and dogs, including sled dogs, is that wolves prefer the company of wolves.

Sled dogs, these beautiful, loving animals, have all the attributes of other domesticated dogs and prefer the company of people. They are, however, predators and have been bred pure for three thousand years, bringing attributes that are not familiar to us—the total concentration and single-mindedness of the predator.

The Currumpaw huskies loved each other with a strong bond and loved the pack. They loved being together, mushing, and every little experience we had. But huskies fight. When huskies fight, they make the most horrible and vicious sounds, and the fights are aggressive. They would fight over anything—even who would get to sniff a blade of grass first.

Fights maintain the pack's order. Leto, the Beta, was the strongest and most aggressive, but Tasha, the Alpha, was highly intelligent with stunning athletic prowess. Fights between the Alpha and Beta were rare, and Tasha was non-confrontational with Leto. Sometimes, when Leto was in the mood to start a fight, Tasha would walk by, turning her head away to avoid eye contact. This showed respect to Leto's position without submitting, giving Leto even greater confidence as the Alpha.

Ici and Leto were always together, always getting into something. They had the type of friendship we all long for, loving every minute of every day together—they were littermates. But sled dogs must follow their instincts, and the two would often fight. Ici was no match for the powerful Leto but wouldn't stand down, usually losing within the first few seconds. Sometimes, Leto had to pin her down until she totally submitted, but she never hurt Ici.

One beautiful Thanksgiving day after a substantial snowfall, I let Leto and Ici play outside. They often spent a lot of time outside, especially when there was nice snow to run and play in. Leto and Ici got into a fight, and of course, Leto was the victor. The fight happened outside without my knowledge. There were no serious injuries except for a few small teeth marks. Ici had a puncture on the top of her head that hurt a little. As it healed, scar tissue formed under her scalp, causing her head to swell like a big balloon. It almost looked funny, but Ici was obviously uncomfortable. The pack's veterinarian, Dr. Wolf, treated her, and everything turned out fine. But huskies remember. From that day on, Ici held a grudge against Leto, and the two had to be separated, unable to be left alone together. It broke my heart to see them apart because they had been such good friends and packmates. At least they were okay together in the house, where play was minimal, and no fighting was allowed. Even after this, Ici and Leto would often huddle together napping.

Blanca was the Omega. She was a big dog and fought dirty. All the Currumpaw sled dogs were actually afraid of her. She was the Omega because she chose to be; she wasn't smart enough to have a higher place in the pack. As the Omega, she would submit to each of the other huskies, putting her tail between her legs, head down, and licking their lips while whining, confirming their higher places in the pack.

When sled dogs fight, like wolves, rarely is there any type of injury. Blanca didn't fight to change her position in the pack; she fought simply because she could—and liked to. If two huskies got into a fight, she would sometimes run towards the fight and join in. This annoyed me as well as the fighting huskies, making breaking up a three-way fight much more difficult. I could pull one off, only to have the first dog jump back in, creating a vicious and endless cycle.

Brandenburg didn't like to fight, even though he was by far the biggest. One day, Leto jumped him. Brandenburg, with a look of absolute horror and terror on his face, stood on his hind legs, backed up against a fence, unable to believe she jumped him. He wouldn't fight back. Brandenburg was sweet and loving beyond imagination. I scolded Leto, and she sat with a sorrowful look, realizing what she had done.

The one thing mushers hate the most is "dog box fights." Sled dogs travel to races in trucks with dog boxes integrated into their sides. Often, mushers put two dogs in each box. Suddenly, you hear that terrible sound—a dog fight in the box. You have no choice but to stick your arm in blindly and pull one out, surely being bitten accidentally each time.

The huskies don't mean to bite you, but the fights are so fast and furious that they bite at anything. The few times I was bitten, the dog that bit me accidentally knew it and would sit with a sorrowful look, feeling really bad. The bites don't hurt much and are never so bad as to cause serious injuries—this level of control is instinctual to them. Fighting is not the hunt; fighting is the way of the pack.

I never lost my temper with the dogs because they never really did anything wrong—fighting is part of what makes sled dogs what they are. Fighting is part of what gives them the fortitude to endure the extreme difficulties of the trail and is the true test of maintaining an appropriate position in the pack. The order of the pack is strong and constantly validating itself.

Chapter 13 – On the Trail

Huskies thrive when running at night, guided by their keen sense of smell and comforted by the cooler temperatures. Our longer runs, often exceeding thirty miles, were always night journeys. The stillness of the night and the ambient light reflecting off the snow illuminated the trail perfectly. Under a high moon, the trail was as bright as day, casting sharp shadows of the team.

One of the most memorable aspects of mushing was bringing the dogs to their positions on the sled's gang line one by one. Initially, I would bring out Tasha first. She would keep tension on the gang line, which connected and held all the dogs together, while I fetched the others. The moment I brought out the second dog, they would begin singing excitedly, with yelps, howls, and barks, eager for the mush. Blanca, in particular, would never stop her endless chorus of "yaaa eeeh hooo waah rouw rouw," which was quite amusing. Leto and Blanca would leap forward with all their might, thinking they could get the sled moving, but the sled was anchored in the ice or secured to an immovable object with a “snub line.” Their jumping only sent them airborne, landing right back where they started. Tasha would often look annoyed as the extra tension on the gang line tugged at her collar, disrupting her own singing and whining.

Each dog’s song grew louder as more were hitched to the gang line. When Brandenburg was finally brought out, the excitement peaked, for they knew the mush was imminent. A husky’s patience vanishes in the face of what they love most. With the forward command “Let’s go,” the loud yelping and howling would cease, replaced by the sound of the sled’s runners gliding on the snow and the palpable energy of the pack. Speed and silence. Mushers have a favorite saying: “Run silent, run dogs.”

After every run, I would rub each husky’s ruff, the thick fur around their neck, and pet their heads, praising them as good sled dogs. They didn't need the praise, for they had done what they loved and were born to do, but the joyous greetings reinforced the pack's togetherness and sense of purpose.

I always ensured not to overwork the Currumpaws, giving them a full day of rest between long mushes. This allowed their bodies to strengthen like athletes. After long runs, they received extra food to support their muscle development. They never ran tired, which was key to their success in races.

Our favorite trail was a five-mile-long path near the huskies' land, offering stunning views, especially at night. One night, after the snow had hardened into ice, we ran the ten miles out and back in under thirty minutes. After the exhilarating run, I praised each husky as usual. Running the dogs was always thrilling and a true blessing.

The five-mile trail extended much further, crossing a busy state road and continuing through a new housing development before re-entering the woods. One winter night, I decided to venture beyond our usual turnaround point. Crossing roads at night was easier due to less traffic and the visibility of headlights. However, when we reached a parking lot before the road, I realized the sled brake was ineffective on the sheer ice created by the day's car traffic.

Despite my efforts, the brake failed to slow the team. I commanded Tasha to stop, but lead dogs rarely understand this command without the sled brake's reinforcement. My fear for the huskies' safety grew as we rapidly approached the road. In a moment of clarity, Tasha sensed the urgency in my voice, digging her feet into the ice and yanking Ici to a stop. The team collided, and I grabbed the neckline to secure them. I praised Tasha, who stood with a serious expression, trying to understand my fear. A good lead dog always brings the team home.

One winter, I took the team over a frozen lake, a risky venture as thin ice could be deadly. The ice seemed thick, and we enjoyed the open ice field until I noticed the snow darkening, indicating weaker ice. Tasha sensed the danger, leading the team in a wide arc to find solid ice and safely returning us to shore. I never dared the ice again.

Brandenburg, our first lead dog, had a keen sense of the trail, avoiding soft ice and other hazards. In those days, Tasha ran lead next to him, while Ici, still learning, was paired with Leto in the wheel position, with Blanca running swing alone.

Once, while mushing young Currumpaws in a state forest, a gang line swivel failed, splitting the team. The lead trio sped off, ignoring my commands to return. With temperatures dropping, I returned to camp with Ici and Blanca, fearing for the missing huskies. A park ranger found them, leading them back attached to his snowmobile. The ranger, moved by the experience, later invited us to film a promotional video, showcasing the Currumpaws' splendor.

In the past, park rangers used dog teams, but snowmobiles had since replaced them. The ranger's joy at working with the huskies highlighted the timeless bond between humans and sled dogs.

Racing didn't provide as many memorable stories as everyday

mushing, except for the thrill of high speeds. Races ranged from single-dog events for children to six-dog classes for experienced mushers. The Currumpaws quickly proved their speed in training, and in their first major race, they dominated the three-dog class despite challenging conditions, winning by over eight minutes. They then placed second in the four-dog class, with Tasha motivating the team.

Spectators, especially the Amish, loved the races. An Amish race across their land brought the community together, enjoying the spectacle. The Amish are familiar with the bond between humans and animals related to the sled dog sport.

The Currumpaws may not have understood their victories, but they loved running and serving me. Each race was perfect for them, as it was for me, and I thought they were perfect too.

Chapter 14 – The Cycle of Life

Something happened to Leto; she started to lose weight. I began giving her insulin shots, and she needed to go out every two hours. At night, she would wake me silently by moving over to me and quietly sitting next to me while I slept. This gentle nudge was enough to wake me, and I would take her out every two hours, every night, for a year. During this time, her love for me seemed to grow even stronger—an incredible loyalty. She showed it to me with her eyes. When I went to the door to let her out, she would look up at me with the most beautiful adoration. I could have separated Leto by placing her and one of the other huskies in the kennel room, but I preferred to wake up and take care of my pack rather than isolating Leto and denying her the pleasure of bonding with the pack during sleep. I wanted her to spend her nights in togetherness with all the huskies, comforted by the rhythmic concert of their breathing.

As time went on, Leto's body continued to fail. Her ears, once sharp to detect danger, were no longer as acute. Her eyes, which had embraced the wonders of the world, grew cloudy. The muscles that once gave her great strength grew smaller and weaker yet still carried her with pride like no other. But her heart grew stronger, and her face became more beautiful than ever. I would watch her go outside by herself, and with absolute heartbreak, I would think, "Oh my poor Leto."

Throughout her entire life, she fought until the end. She died young. Why her? Why the strongest? Why the one who loved life more than any other? When she looked up at me with those adoring eyes, she truly believed I could make everything all right. Part of me believes that because she believed it, I somehow failed her. I could never make things all right for her.

Bearing the sorrow of Leto's passing was difficult, but I believe with all my heart that I was not alone in recognizing the significance of this great animal's life. At the very moment of Leto's death, I heard the most disturbing sound—a siren, then a loud screech and a boom. I walked to the front of my property and saw the dead body of a deer struck by a speeding police car. The impact had flung it through the air, landing on my lawn—Leto's home. The deer, part of the symbiotic relationship with Leto, a predator, had with nature, seemed to symbolize the Earth mourning her passing and recognizing my loyalty during her sickness. The deer spirit sacrificed a life in remembrance of Leto. I buried Leto on her land and wrote on her collar, "protector of life, lust for life as no other," capturing her brave experiences not all told in this story.

I buried her in a special place where she liked to gaze over her land, watching the rolling orchards and the woods. She rests where she can see the beautiful sunset over the orchards and where the deer, the fox, and all the wild animals pass by. The four huskies watched as I gently lowered her into her grave—they knew where she was.

The pack's order is strong, with each member holding a special and important place. Leto was the protector of the pack. At home, she slept in her private place under a small table. She would wake at short intervals, touring the house, checking doors, windows, and anywhere a scent might indicate an intruder. She ensured each pack member's safety before returning to her private place to relax. Even though she was buried in this beautiful place on her land, with the occasional company of passing wildlife, it broke my heart to think of her sleeping there without her pack—alone.

Chapter 15 – A Husky Howls

Wolves and huskies howl for many reasons, some of which remain a mystery to us. However, we do know that they howl to locate members of their pack and that they howl in unison, each in a different pitch, creating a harmonious lupine chord that makes the pack seem larger than it is.

Blanca had lost her daughter and friend, and after Leto was buried, she didn't like to come into the house. She would sit outside near Leto's grave, her little girl. Huskies howl, but Blanca would sit by Leto's grave and let out these awful, long, mournful howls—remembering, missing her little girl, and perhaps hoping that her Leto would return to her. If that was so, she never lost that hope. Perhaps one day, she will be reunited with Leto.

Brandenburg was the oldest and passed away a few months later. His was a happy and joyful life. He was the sweetest dog to walk this

Earth. The three huskies watched me as I buried my buddy on his land next to Leto. I placed my hand on the heavy cut stone that marked where Leto had been sleeping without her pack, looked through the Earth toward her, and gave her just a little sad smile. From this day on, Leto does not sleep alone.

Chapter 16 – Of Currumpaw's Natasha Ko

Tasha was my favorite; throughout her life, she barely did anything wrong. Like her legendary grandfather, Innisfree's Pegasus, she was never in trouble. Tasha was always by my side. Sometimes, she would take this further and overly submit to me in both a dominating and submissive posture. While I sat, she would often climb up onto me, forepaws first, and lick my face repeatedly. She especially liked to sneak up on me if I were lying on the floor watching television. She would pounce, holding my neck down with one forepaw and my forehead with the other, then start licking my face.

Siberian Huskies are beautiful, but Tasha was uncommonly so. She stood strong and proud, her strength and beauty shining through - she was the Alpha female. Tasha loved playing fetch with her little yellow football. She would chase and return it tirelessly. If I threw it for her to catch, she would throw it back into my hand. If I didn't play fetch with her, she would bring me the football and force it into my hand.

Tasha was my best lead dog, and I suspect one of the best that ever lived. Once, while crossing a lake with Tasha leading, the ice began to break; Tasha quickly steered the team across safe ice. Many times, we faced danger on the trail; a good lead dog, she could always sense danger and find a safe path. Tasha always brought the team home.

The native people say there are many trails in life; the only good trail to follow is that of a good human being. My lead dog reminded me of this on every mush; it will be difficult to follow her trail, her great courage, her joy for life, her love for the pack, and the love she had for me.

Tasha, being the great lead dog that she was, had a sense of all things around her; she needed to be in control. One day, Blanca jumped her and tore Tasha's lower left eyelid. I took Tasha to Dr. Wolf, who stitched her up. Dr. Wolf, not the local veterinarian but the caretaker of the Currumpaw pack, had to anesthetize Tasha. She woke up in my living room with a look of total confusion. From that day on, she did not like to go into any room in the vet's office.

All the mushers were jealous of Tasha and of the Currumpaw wins. I didn't have the huskies to race but to share my life with, experience the behavior of the pack firsthand, and run them. Racing was just a way for them to see other dogs and be admired by spectators. Because sled dogs were difficult to control, they were prohibited from walking off-lead at races and weren't supposed to leave the staging area. But the race officials were proud of Tasha, and I would rub salt in the mushers' wounds by taking Tasha with me everywhere - off-lead.

At one race, I walked into a cabin, leaving her outside on a deck. When I returned, she stood there with a loving and content look. Six or seven small children, each only two or three years old, surrounded her, each with a hand on her, petting and touching her. Tasha stood there smiling - I will always remember her this way.

When Tasha was barely an adolescent, a friend left something at my house, so I took Tasha with me to return it to a dance studio. Tasha was instantly surrounded by ballet dancers doting on her. Tasha, distracted and smiling, didn't hear me say it was time to go. I left anyway, thinking it would be a good lesson for her as a lead dog to keep her attention on me. As I walked away, I looked back and saw Tasha shooting out the door, sliding sideways on the slippery floor with a comical look of worry and focus. For the rest of her life, she never lost focus on me and would run to my side with just the wave of my finger, looking at me with happiness and pride, hoping I would ask her to do something.

Tasha, the Alpha female, had a thirst for the hunt. While mushing, deer would often pass, and Tasha wanted dearly to chase them. A good lead dog, she fought her instincts and kept mushing, turning her head repeatedly to watch the deer. One night, while walking on the huskies' land, Tasha bolted toward a herd of deer and disappeared into the woods. She didn't catch any deer but found her way home quickly.

The next day, Tasha walked at my side with a new pride. She had pursued the herd, fulfilling a part of her hopes and dreams. I was happy for her. Tasha was uncommonly intelligent, which is evident in everyday life. When she wanted to come inside, she would knock at the door. When Blanca was a puppy, Tasha would open her cage by flipping the latch and sliding it over, letting Blanca out faster than I could.

When Tasha grew old and became sick, we had several extra months together. We played many fetch games with her little yellow football. Late in the winter, we were blessed with fresh snowfall, and I took Tasha for a walk off-lead across the snow. Blanca and Ici stood watching as we returned to the house. It struck me that soon, it would be just Blanca and Ici together. It was the last walk in the snow my lead dog would ever make.

When her time came, I fell asleep next to Tasha on the floor, her warm fur pressing against my face. Her breathing was heavy as we went to sleep. I dreaded the next day, Tasha's beautiful and athletic body failing. I would call Dr. Wolf to help her sleep.

I woke up the next day, and there she was, snuggled next to me with a look of happiness and contentment. Even in passing, she was no trouble. I sat up, stroking her beautiful fur, remembering all the wonderful experiences and her love for me. I held her and sang her song into her ear, whispering the words I dreaded, "Farewell my Tasha, my Natasha Ko; I will feel so alone without you at my side."

I buried her on her land next to her love, with her favorite toy. Blanca and Ici watched with a shocked look of responsibility. The Alpha, their leader, was gone. I miss her and long for the sight of her gazing into my eyes. My life is so much less without her love.

Chapter 17 – The Perfect Sled Dog

Blanca was all sled dog, mischievous and hilarious. When people visited, she would talk to them, "rouw row rah rooh." If she could, she would lick you with her big, sloppy, wet tongue, especially after drinking water, to make it extra wet, enjoying the annoyed reaction of the recipient. Then, she would go back to her water dish and lay with her snout in the water, blowing bubbles. Blanca was a very happy husky who could always find a way to amuse herself.

She loved attention more than any of the other huskies. When I petted her, I would often rub her ruff on both sides, and Blanca would purr, rest the top of her head between my feet, and roll head over heels toward me, flopping right over. She was always a clown. Most of the huskies were not too concerned with other people, focusing their love and attention on me or the Currumpaw pack. Being the Omega and the mischievous fighter she was, if you started to pet one of the huskies, Blanca would come running and push the other husky away to hog all the attention. Blanca loved everybody and may have been the happiest sled dog that ever lived.

On the trail, she was all business. When I ran all five dogs, Blanca would run in the swing position, in the middle of the gang line between the lead and wheel pairs. I placed her there because nothing could distract her from staying on the trail, not misbehaving dogs, not even deer on the trail. She made mushing the full team easier. At home, she would spend hours grooming her feet, biting them, pulling her paw off the floor, ensuring they were in perfect order for the next mush.

After Tasha passed, Blanca sat by the huskies' graves, letting out long, mournful howls. She stopped spending too much time outside and began staying by me. I gave her lots of extra attention, and she took Tasha's place at my side. Blanca began sleeping next to me, huddled next to Ici on my left. And I would slip my right hand under her, and she would sleep on my hand the rest of the night. Was she taking Tasha's place, or was she keeping close to avoid losing any other pack members? I will never know this because I didn't have enough time to learn all that she felt; Blanca fell ill suddenly.

I honored this great sled dog by washing and grooming her feet one last time. I buried her with the other three huskies next to Leto and Brandenburg. I buried her with her favorite bone. The only remaining Currumpaw, Ici - Currumpaw's Ice Dancer, stood and watched me with remembering eyes as I lowered Blanca into her grave.

Chapter 18 – At Heaven's Gate

When I assembled the team in those early years, I often thought about how wonderful it would be to live with the pack and spend my life with them. Sled dogs can live well over ten years, and having the Currumpaws felt so permanent. Those years, however, passed in an instant.

The Chukchi believe that at heaven's gates, all the sled dogs that ever lived stand together, and anyone who did not treat their sled dogs well shall not pass. Your sled dogs wait for you there, and the way you treated your huskies in this life determines your place in heaven. These little dogs possess a courage not often seen in our comfortable world. Who better could God have chosen to stand guard at His gates?

After burying Blanca, I looked up at Ici. Seeing her standing there all alone without her pack, I felt great sympathy for her and cried out to her with all my heart, from the depth of my soul, which had been so enlightened and blessed by the experience of living with the Currumpaws: "Oh poor Ici, your huskies are gone."

I stood there with Ici and looked up to the heavens where the sled dogs stand at the gates. I told my huskies that Blanca was coming.

I told Leto to play king of the mountain with her, to remember to bark and taunt each other, dropping on their forearms while standing on their hind legs, one husky charging suddenly towards the other—the other bolting away, laughing.

I told Brandenburg to go sniff her and give her that look of contentment as he always did, smiling with his eyes half-closed.

I told Tasha to pounce on Blanca the way she always did, with Blanca trying to bolt past her, laughing and scooting as they do; Blanca's back legs beginning to overtake her front legs, her butt and tail down; Tasha standing defiantly while Blanca bolted past, finally leaping through the air in a graceful arch, biting Blanca on the back of the neck.

I will try to walk that road to heaven, and should I be so blessed as to make it to its gates and see my Tasha and her Currumpaw pack, along with all the Chukchi sled dogs as far as the eye can see, I will desire to go no further. I will stand with them.

I can borrow, with a heavy heart, an expression from the Texas cowboys who claim that it was a cruel God that made the horse's life shorter than the cowboy's. It was a cruel God that made the huskies' lives shorter than mine.

Chapter 19 - The Order of the Pack is Strong

The order of the pack was strong, and each member had a special and important place. Tasha and Brandenburg, the Alpha pair, Leto, the Beta, and Blanca, the Omega. It was partially this order that made the Currumpaw Siberians what they were.

This order was most apparent when we would return from a mush. Thirsty, the huskies preferred drinking water from their dish in the house. While writing this book, I remembered how fascinating this ritual was. I would fill the large water bowl, and each time, the same thing would happen.

The huskies would queue up in single file, in the order of the pack. Brandenburg would drink first, then Tasha, Leto, Ici, and finally Blanca. They stood in line patiently, fighting only to validate the pack order, confirming it with fascinating and polite gestures. Today, when I make dinner, I first fill Ici's dish with her favorite food, then I sit and dine, Ici lying on the floor next to me. When I'm finished, she'll walk to her dish and eat her food.

Sometimes, I sit and relax in our den or read a book, and I will look up to find Ici staring at me. Being predators and pack members, staring was something the huskies rarely did.

Staring is not something pack members do, as it creates a challenge with the dog being stared at. Sometimes, the huskies, especially Tasha, would stare at me with loving adoration. But Ici's stoic gaze was different. She would do this often. At these times, her stares were not of loving adoration. What does she see? I remembered the night it was forty below zero, and Brandenburg wouldn't come into the house. He stood out in the bitter cold, looking off into the land, then stared out the window once he came back in. Ici is a spirit dog, and I wondered if my huskies were watching me through her eyes.

As Ici grew older, she often went into the kennel room where I used to keep the huskies when I was away. The kennel room was in a far corner of the house that we rarely passed during a day's activities. It was an empty space filled with ghosts of days past, days that would never return. Afterwards, Ici would look towards the kennel room from a distance, tilting her head back with her nose in the air, sniffing. I never knew for certain why she would go there, but when she began sniffing the air from a distance, I realized she was checking if one of the huskies had been hiding there all this time or remembering those wonderful days when the pack was together, sleeping there while waiting for me to return home from work.

Other times, Ici would ask to be let out shortly after she had already been outside. When the pack was together, this was common because they wanted to go out on the land and play. She would ask me to let her out, go up to the special opening that would let her outside, and then suddenly stop and stare out at the land. She would put her head down and slowly walk back to me; there was no longer anything out there for her. Her huskies and playmates were gone, and she would come back in because she had an important place at my side.

Ici and I walked to the beginning of the huskies' favorite trail, that fast, long, five-mile trail. The trail runs straight and is high above the land. The land slopes off from each side of the trail, and to its west side is a steep wooded ravine. The trail is absolutely beautiful, and I possess the most wonderful memories of the huskies mushing this trail. I look down the long, straight trail that seems to come to a point in the distance, and I remember how fast we could travel, the trees moving by, the sound of the runners, the silent sound of running the dogs. Most of all, I remember the exuberance of the team as they waited to start, the joy that came from the team as we sped along the trail, and their fulfillment in doing what they thought was so necessary to me.

I worry for Ici. When she looks around her land, she does not see the comforting sight of her pack, of her kind. She is the last of the Currumpaws.

Chapter 20 – Of Dr. Bruce Wolf, the Absent Pack Member

When I embarked on the journey of raising the Currumpaws, I was well-versed in dog training and knowledgeable about huskies and dog sledding. I also had considerable experience in caring for dogs' health, though it paled in comparison to that of a veterinarian.

Located on the far side of the city was a veterinary practice run by Dr. Wolf. He was a gentleman with twinkling eyes, a love for both people and animals and qualities rarely found in today's world. Dr. Wolf was incredibly generous and possessed an insatiable thirst for knowledge to enhance his skills and abilities. His actions were always compassionate and generous, and this kindness was undoubtedly returned to him daily because, as they say, there is no gift like giving. Although it was inconvenient for me to drive across the city to see him, his unmatched talents made him the perfect caretaker for the

Currumpaw pack's health.

Dr. Wolf treated a variety of animals and had a special affinity for Rottweilers. However, when he realized he had the chance to care for and learn from the Currumpaws, which he referred to as "real working dogs," he embraced the challenge and opportunity with great enthusiasm. It struck me as almost humorous that a doctor named "Wolf" would end up caring for the Currumpaws.

Dr. Wolf devoted himself entirely to the Currumpaws. No one could have provided better care, more intelligent diagnoses, or more kindness to the pack. Sometimes, I had to leave one of the huskies overnight at the clinic, and he would "borrow" that husky, taking it home to observe and enjoy. I'm glad he did this because, despite all his time and effort, he didn't experience the same overwhelming joy I received from living with the pack. By taking them home during their times of sickness, he could share in a bit of the joy of the Currumpaws. He always felt their pain and hardships and later mourned each one's death as if they were his own huskies.

Chapter 21 – Evening

As evening falls, I unwind in my usual way, with Ici lying in her favorite spot next to the sled that revolutionized the mushing world. She stretches out, her head touching the runners of the sled, and soon falls asleep. While she sleeps, her legs twitch, and she lets out little yelps. I wish I could join her in her dreams, where she surely must be running with a sled, her Currumpaw pack pulling on the neckline attached to Tasha when she received the "haw" command. In her dreams, she's playing with her beloved Leto and surrounded by all the Currumpaw sled dogs, her family, and her pack.

Morning arrives, and Ici wakes up from her sleep on my left side, near the spot at the corner of the bed where Leto once slept. In this way, she takes Leto's place, holding on to the pack's memories. I miss the days when Ici slept over my right leg, and I would wake up feeling her head resting on my thigh. This was her place when the pack was whole. Despite my deep understanding of the pack's ways, I still long for the days when Ici slept over my right leg.

With Leto and the rest of the pack gone, my resilient little Ici has taken their place, stepping into the role of the missing Alpha, Tasha. The lower pack members, including Leto, could enjoy a pleasure that Tasha never did because this was not for their leader. The huskies would often huddle together when they rested, snuggled up to keep each other warm, even in the summer. When Ici was a pack member, she would sleep over my right leg every night. Now, as the Alpha, she sleeps at my left, without the comfort of the huddle, maintaining the stoic aloofness required of a leader. Though I wish it were different, Ici fulfills her life as a pack member, embracing her role.

It's Sunday, and Ici will have fun. She rides in my truck, standing behind me with her head slightly out the window, occasionally touching her nose to my cheek. I glance over at her, seeing the splendor of what she is—standing proudly, carrying the experiences of living with her pack, the love she gave, and the love she received. Ici stands proud, unlike any common animal, with a piece of each Currumpaw living in her heart, glowing with pride and the wonder of her life experiences. She knows she has lived as God intended—serving the People and living with the Pack, true to her essence, true to all that sled dogs ever were and are.

Unlike the Siberian Huskies we often see with their owners, Ici stands with a special pride, a light glowing from her eyes. Ici is a sled dog and a lead dog who has followed the best trail in life.

Now, with fewer dogs, Ici gets to do things she couldn't do before. She joins me for family dinners, receives treats, and has lots of fun—after all, fun is what a sled dog's life is about. She goes to sleep happy, snuggled up on my left, knowing that the Chukchis, my totem—the wolf spirit—and all the Chukchi sled dogs at the gates of heaven are smiling at her.

Ici is healthy and will likely live long, maintaining the strong order of the pack. To her, there are still two of us, and she won't want to leave me alone.

Chapter 22 – The Survival of the Pack

The instinct for the survival of the pack is deeply ingrained, and the legacy of the Currumpaws lives on through Ici. She enhances my joy of living with them and my experience of being blessed by the company and love of a sled dog. However, things have changed, and now Ici does not always wake on my left, nor does she wake on my right as she did for most of her life. Ici possesses a remarkable gift of empathy, sensing what people feel, and most importantly, she can feel what I feel.

There are moments, in certain situations, when Ici wakes in a special place, waiting for an assurance that her pack will endure. It is due to the fault of my own heart that she does this, and I dislike these times when she is not by my side.

I will let Ici live out the rest of her days with the hope she demonstrates by where she sometimes wakes. Unlike the story of the Currumpaws, this is a tale of her heartbreak and hope, and because of my love for her, it is one I can never share. I will let Ici keep her hope, and I will continue to learn from her as I have experienced the resilience of the Chukchi Sled Dog. I am fortunate to witness that their strengths truly exist in this world. We should all learn from them: loyalty, unconditional love, joy, a love for life and the Earth, and the determination to never quit or give up hope. These traits are immortalized in the statue of Balto in Central Park. I promise Ici that I will hold on to hope as well and, God willing, that her hopes might be fulfilled in the many ways she needs.

Chapter 23 – Another Currumpaw Morning

The sun rises, and I wake as the light beams through the window and shines on Ici. I feel her warm, furry presence to my left; she's still sleeping. She's had a wondrous life and has been going to sleep even happier these days, perhaps because her hopes and dreams have finally been realized - Ici's hope that her pack will live on. I move closer to my Pretty, put my arms around her, holding her tight, feeling her soft fur, and inhaling the wonderful clean fur scent that huskies have. I lay with her, holding her for a long while because that day, I didn't want to get out of bed either.

I head downstairs to my spacious family room and lay on the couch for a while, reminiscing about my huskies and the endless joyful days with the Currumpaws. I remember their playful antics, their passion for mushing, their love for each other, and the love they had for me. I think of all our wonderful experiences on the trail, their courage, and their stunning strength and beauty.

The family room is adorned with artifacts reflecting the sled dog breeding cultures of the American Eskimo and the Chukchi and many wonderful items collected or won during our years of dog sledding. It's not just a family room; it's the den of the Currumpaws. This is where they spent their time while in the house. One of Tasha's little yellow footballs still sits on the windowsill. Pictures of the Currumpaws are everywhere, capturing their puppyhood, their personalities, and the energy and joyous enthusiasm of the mush. There are two picture albums, beautifully bound in rich walnut, sitting on the wet bar, chronologies of the pack's lives from their births to their glorious days on the trail. There are even pictures of Tasha's last walk in the snow and the poignant images of Ici and Blanca standing alone together, waiting for our return.

This room is also where the Currumpaws' racing sled rests, forever still without its team. In the sled's basket lie the retired harnesses and sled dog collars of my huskies. The neon-colored harnesses are laid out next to each other, still glowing with the energy of the dogs that once so proudly wore them. I walk over to where I keep my sled dog equipment, retrieve Ici's harness and collar, and lay them down on the sled with the others. Now, my sled is complete.

I step outside, attend to the necessary tasks of the day, and then return to the house to get my precious Pretty. Ici and I go outside on the huskies' land, walking to where my huskies rest on the earth.

I place my hand on each of the large sandstones marking my huskies' resting spots and ask them each for something different. I ask Brandenburg to help me with patience and contentment, Leto to continue to protect me and teach me courage, Blanca to help me find joy, and Tasha to guide me so that I may always choose the only good trail in life.

We walk to the spot right next to where Ici's beloved Leto lies. I look to my left at the empty space on the huskies' land, once filled with the joy, antics, and life of the Currumpaw pack. There are no huskies watching as I tremble while gently lowering my dearest Ici, my Pretty, into her grave.

Now, Ici and Leto are sleeping side by side once again, and my huskies are resting, flanked by my two great lead dogs. All my huskies are together again. My land is where my dead lay buried; I pray I never have to leave this land that is theirs.

There is a mushers' legend that says your huskies lay sleeping, waiting for you, and when you come across them, they greet you with the joy that accompanies every meeting and the beginning of every mush. Together again, they pull your sled through and into heaven. I miss my life with the Currumpaws, and I miss each of them. It will not be possible for me to raise a pack the way the Currumpaws were raised, and I will never again feel the love that poured from each of their eyes. The Currumpaw pack lives on in my heart. From where the sun now stands, I will mush no more forever.

I will try to walk the path to heaven and live my life as God intended so that I may be so blessed one day that the Currumpaws will awaken and we will be reunited. Tasha and her pack will pull my sled on that final journey.

I look up to heaven, where the Chukchi dogs stand at its gates, and imagine Ici arriving, seeing all my huskies joyfully running up to her with their noses touching and tails wagging, as is the pack's greeting. Suddenly, all the Chukchi sled dogs turn and look toward the gates, smiling as huskies do. Someone is peering through the gates, looking toward His huskies, which stand as far as the eye can see and smile back, knowing that once again, He did Good. A good lead dog always brings the team home.

Acknowledgements & References

1. Currumpaw; The Story of the Currumpaw Wolf: Outlaw Wolves – From "Of Wolves and Men," By Barry Lopez

"One of the more poignant stories about an outlaw or renegade wolf concerns that Currumpaw Wolf of northern New Mexico and his mate Blanca, who were killed in 1894 by the naturalist Ernest Thompson Seton.

Seton, called in by a concerned rancher who was a friend, tried every sort of set he could devise to no avail. Each time, the Currumpaw Wolf would dig up and spring the traps or pointedly ignore them.

One evening, Seton set out to concoct the be-all-andend-all of baits: "Acting on the hint of an old trapper, I melted some cheese together with the kidney fat of a freshly killed heifer, stewing it in a china dish, and cutting it with a bone knife to avoid the taint of metal. When the mixture was cool, I cut it into lumps and making a hole in the side of each lump. I inserted a large dose of strychnine and cyanide, contained in a capsule that was impermeable by any odor; finally, I sealed the holes with pieces of the cheese itself. During the whole process, I wore a pair of gloves, steeped in the hot blood of the heifer, and even avoided breathing on the baits. When all was ready, I put them in a raw-hide bag rubbed all over with blood and rode forth dragging the liver and kidneys of the beef at the end of a rope. With this I made a ten-mile circuit, dropping a bait at each quarter mile and taking the utmost care, always not to touch any with my hands."

Seton's caution and arcane science were techniques much praised by wolfers of the time. The Currumpaw Wolf, for his part, carefully gathered four of the baits in a pile and defecated on them.

The female wolf, Blanca, was finally caught in a steel trap in the spring of 1894. Seton and a companion approached the wolf on horseback. "Then followed the inevitable tragedy, the idea of which I shrank from afterward more than at the time. We threw a lasso over the neck of the doomed wolf and strained our horses in opposite directions until the blood burst from her mouth, her eyes glazed, her limbs stiffened, and then fell limp."

The dead female was taken back to the ranch. The male, abandoning all his former caution, followed her and, the next day, stepped into a nest of traps set around the ranch buildings. He was chained up and left for the night but was found dead in the morning without a wound or any sign of a struggle. Seton, deeply moved by what happened, placed his dead body in the shed next to Blanca's.

The price offered to the man who would kill the Currumpaw Wolf was one thousand dollars. Seton never says whether he took it."

In hindsight, we know that it was not just the Currumpaw Wolf that dug up the traps and made insult of the poisons left for his pack—it was the Alpha pair, the Wolf, and his mate Blanca. The Alpha male brings strength and confidence to the pack, but it was the intelligence, and vigilant passion, and concern for the well-being of the pack that came from the Alpha female that caused many of the events that saved the Currumpaw Wolf's pack.

The order of the pack is strong, with each member having its own special and important place. Wolf packs grow to a certain size, a size that is dictated by the resources of their territory. Each member has an important place in the hunt, and the pack cannot support the weak, the sick, or the very old. Somehow, wolves communicate a strategy that is played out during the hunt—it is not known how such abstract concepts are communicated among wolves.

Knowing this, there is a lesson for us all. In the late nineteen eighties, a wolf biologist observed a pack that included a very old female.

Somewhat healthy, the old female had no teeth— broken from years of hunting and deteriorated from age. Teeth are critical to a successful hunt. By watching this pack, the biologist realized that she, too, possessed something crucial to the survival of the pack and the success of the hunt—she possessed knowledge.

****

After the serum run, Seppala toured North America with Togo and many of his sled dogs. They ran in many races, winning most of them. Togo retired to the farm of Mrs. Elizabeth Ricker, who was instrumental in bringing the breed to its present state of popularity. Togo spent the rest of his life in her wonderful surroundings, and she paid special attention to him. Togo died on December 5, 1929.

****

2. The Amish refer to non-Amish cultures as "the English".

****

3. My Land Lies Where My Dead Lay Buried

This phrase is taken from the words of Crazy Horse, the Sioux warrior. Upon the final defeat of the Indian Nation in 1877, the remaining warriors were taken to a fort to wait to be moved to a reservation. For all the courage and heartbreak of the native Americans, the soldiers mocked the warriors, who were now heartbroken and forcibly removed from their place in God's plan, the Earth. One soldier recognized Crazy Horse, laughing, and said, "Where's your land now, Crazy Horse?" Crazy Horse turned, extended his arm, and pointed out to the Land, saying, "My land lies where my dead lay buried."

****

4. From Where The Sun Now Stands, I Will Mush No More Forever

This phrase is taken from the words of Chief Joseph, named Hinmaton Kalakitt of the Nez Perce tribe. Defeated, broken-hearted, and removed from their place in God's Land following the great slaughter at Wounded Knee in 1877, the chief surrendered to the American Army on behalf of the native people—speaking not to the conquering American colonel and his officers, but directly to the chiefs of the remaining People:

"I am tired of fighting. Our chiefs are killed. Looking Glass is dead. Toohulhulsote is dead. The old men are all dead. It is the young men who say no and yes. He who led the young men is dead.

It is cold, and we have no blankets. The little children are freezing to death.

My people, some of them, have run away to the hills and have no blankets, no food.

No one knows where they are—perhaps they are freezing to death.

I want to have time to look for my children and see how many of them I can find.

Maybe I shall find them among the dead.

Hear me, my chiefs, I am tired. My heart is sad and sick.

From where the sun now stands, I will fight no more forever."

Chapter 24 – The Trail Continues

My brother Denny never had the chance to publish his book because, on April 30th, 2004, he was tragically killed in a motorcycle accident. During Easter, he was excitedly talking about having a book signing once it was published. He was so pleased with how it turned out and the wonderful feedback he received from family and friends who had read his manuscript. I was fortunate to spend quality time with him during that Easter. We never know when the angel of death will come for us. Denny took care of the pack as they fell ill, keeping them comfortable until the end. Riding his Harley was his preferred mode of transportation, and he passed away doing what he loved.

Denny always had a passion for being in the wind, whether it was driving in the winter with the windows down, skiing, cycling, or riding motorcycles. Now, he has reunited with the huskies at heaven's gate. Together again, Denny is on his sled with Tasha Ko leading the pack on their journey to heaven.

I remember the joy he had while working on his book and the pride he felt in his writing. He was looking forward to sharing his stories with the world. Although he never got to see his book published, his spirit lives on through the memories we shared and the love he had for the pack.

Denny's love for the wind and the open road was evident throughout his life. He found freedom and peace in these moments, and it is fitting that he left this world in such a way. His legacy continues in the hearts of those who knew him and the stories he left behind.

Now, as I think of Denny, I can picture him with the Currumpaws, guiding them through the trails of heaven. His journey did not end with his passing; it continued in a place where he could be free and surrounded by the beloved huskies he cared for so deeply. Denny is now part of the eternal pack, leading them with the same passion and love he had in life.

About the Author

By Al & Grace Abarca

- At 7 years old, he played a duet recital for the Hammond Society.
- High school, he was with the National Ski Patrol @ Brandywine.
- Ohio Region 1975-1976 Ski & Toboggan Competition:
- First Place – Hot Dog Event
- He went on to win many other competitions, which led him to ski with the US Ski Team
- Started Rainbow Freestyle Productions

- Built a mobile carpeted treadmill powered by a 3 hp, 20V motor ski deck.
- Exhibition of freestyle skiing @ Dayton Ski & Winter Sports Fair, many malls • “Winter Dreams Deck Show” @ Cleveland Ski & Winter Sports Fair
- Built a slide at a Lake in Lodi, Ohio, to practice Flipping on skis and landing in water

- Started team Equipe Velo Club member of the U.S. Cycling Federation
- Massillon Bicycle Race Licensed 25 miles 18 & over 3rd Place

- Grand Prix of Cycling Toronto, Canada

MURRAY
MURRAY

The Following Denny won many Ribbons & Metals:

- 1982 The Wildwoods USA Pro AM Bike Race
- 1982 U.S. Cycling Federation District Championship Sr. Men Pursuit • 1983 U.S. Cycling Federation District Championship Sr. Men Kilo

- 1983 U.S. Cycling Federation District Championship Sr. Men
- 1983 U.S. Cycling Federation Sr. men Sprints

- 1984 Lehigh County Velodrome USCF
- 1984 U.S. Cycling Federation District Championship Sr. Men Pt. Race • 1984 U.S. Cycling Federation District Championship Sr. Men Sprints • 1985 U.S. Cycling federation

District Ohio, W. Va., Sr. men Kilo

- 1986 Almost May Day 1st Place Experienced Bike Race

1986 Almost May Day 2nd Place 24 – 29 Bike races

- World Masters "Coupe Du Monde" track Championship Minneapolis & St.

Johann, Austria

- 1989 Ohio Festival State Games
- 1991 Ohio Festival State Games
- 1991 Eden Soy. Saline Bike Criterium-Masters Category 6th Place
- 1992 REVCO Cleveland Criterium
- 1994 Velodrome NSL World Cup
- 1994 Medina YWCA Twin Sizzler Expert Bike Race 1st Place Siberian Husky Club of Greater Cleveland

- Four Ribbons – First, Second & Third Place
- Buckeye Feeds Classic 3 Dog Sled Pure Bred 1st place & 2 Trophies
- 1st Place weight Pull
- Buckeye Feeds Classic Fastest All Siberian Team 3 Dog Class 4 Trophies
- Siberian Husky Club 3rd Fastest 4 Dog Team

Articles Published

- Pollution Engineering October 1998 “Implementing ISO 9000 & ISO 14000 by: Dennis Abarca
- Quality Digest February 1999 “Making the Most of Internal Audits” by: Dennis Abarca
- Environmental Protection November 1998 “A Platform for Pollution Prevention by: Dennis Abarca

www.ingramcontent.com/pod-product-compliance
Ingram Content Group UK Ltd.
Pitfield, Milton Keynes, MK11 3LW, UK
UKHW062301290726
14090UKWH00017B/832

9 798330 300105